Diary 2010

Published by the Natural History Museum, London

The pictures gathered in this diary are prize-winning or commended images from past years of the Wildlife Photographer of the Year competition – the international showcase for the very best photography featuring natural subjects. It is owned by two UK institutions that pride themselves on revealing and championing the diversity of life on Earth: the Natural History Museum and *BBC Wildlife Magazine*.

The origins of the competition go back to 1964, when the magazine was called Animals and there were just 3 categories and about 600 entries. It grew in stature over the years and, in 1984, *BBC Wildlife Magazine* and the Natural History Museum joined forces to create the competition as it is today.

Open to visitors since 1881, the Natural History Museum looks after a world-class collection of 70 million specimens. It is also a leading scientific-research institution, with ground-breaking projects in more than 68 countries. About 300 scientists work at the Museum, researching the valuable collections to better understand life on Earth. Every year more than 3 million visitors, of all ages and levels of interest, are welcomed through the Museum's doors.

Wildlife Photographer of the Year is one of the most popular of the Museum's exhibitions. Visitors come to see breathtaking imagery, but also to understand some of the threats faced by our planet's animals and plants. Understanding and finding ways of conserving the Earth's biodiversity is at the heart of the Museum's work. This exhibition is one way to share that mission with others, encouraging us to see the environment around us with new eyes.

For more than 40 years *BBC Wildlife* has celebrated and shared the miracle and beauty of nature with its readers.

Every issue is packed with inspirational images by the world's best photographers – many of them Wildlife Photographer of the Year award-winners – and informative, entertaining features by experts.

We reveal how to get closer to Britain's magnificent wildlife, enjoy great days out and attract everything from bugs to badgers to your garden. Plus, stay up to date with the latest conservation issues, environmental news and scientific discoveries from around the globe.

To find out more about *BBC Wildlife*, improve your own wildlife photography and enter our reader's competition, visit www.bbcwildlifemagazine.com

2010

JANUARY

wk	M	T	W	Th	F	S	S
1					1	2	3
2	4	5	6	7	8	9	10
3	11	12	13	14	15	16	17
4	18	19	20	21	22	23	24
5	25	26	27	28	29	30	31

FEBRUARY

wk	M	T	W	Th	F	S	S
6	1	2	3	4	5	6	7
7	8	9	10	11	12	13	14
8	15	16	17	18	19	20	21
9	22	23	24	25	26	27	28

MARCH

wk	M	T	W	Th	F	S	S
10	1	2	3	4	5	6	7
11	8	9	10	11	12	13	14
12	15	16	17	18	19	20	21
13	22	23	24	25	26	27	28
14	29	30	31				

APRIL

wk	M	T	W	Th	F	S	S
14				1	2	3	4
15	5	6	7	8	9	10	11
16	12	13	14	15	16	17	18
17	19	20	21	22	23	24	25
18	26	27	28	29	30		

MAY

wk	M	T	W	Th	F	S	S
18						1	2
19	3	4	5	6	7	8	9
20	10	11	12	13	14	15	16
21	17	18	19	20	21	22	23
22	24	25	26	27	28	29	30
23	31						

JUNE

wk	M	T	W	Th	F	S	S
23		1	2	3	4	5	6
24	7	8	9	10	11	12	13
25	14	15	16	17	18	19	20
26	21	22	23	24	25	26	27
27	28	29	30				

JULY

wk	M	T	W	Th	F	S	S
27				1	2	3	4
28	5	6	7	8	9	10	11
29	12	13	14	15	16	17	18
30	19	20	21	22	23	24	25
31	26	27	28	29	30	31	

AUGUST

wk	M	T	W	Th	F	S	S
31							1
32	2	3	4	5	6	7	8
33	9	10	11	12	13	14	15
34	16	17	18	19	20	21	22
35	23	24	25	26	27	28	29
36	30	31					

SEPTEMBER

wk	M	T	W	Th	F	S	S
36			1	2	3	4	5
37	6	7	8	9	10	11	12
38	13	14	15	16	17	18	19
39	20	21	22	23	24	25	26
40	27	28	29	30			

OCTOBER

wk	M	T	W	Th	F	S	S
40					1	2	3
41	4	5	6	7	8	9	10
42	11	12	13	14	15	16	17
43	18	19	20	21	22	23	24
44	25	26	27	28	29	30	31

NOVEMBER

wk	M	T	W	Th	F	S	S
45	1	2	3	4	5	6	7
46	8	9	10	11	12	13	14
47	15	16	17	18	19	20	21
48	22	23	24	25	26	27	28
49	29	30					

DECEMBER

wk	M	T	W	Th	F	S	S
49			1	2	3	4	5
50	6	7	8	9	10	11	12
51	13	14	15	16	17	18	19
52	20	21	22	23	24	25	26
1	27	28	29	30	31		

2011

JANUARY

wk	M	T	W	Th	F	S	S
1						1	2
2	3	4	5	6	7	8	9
3	10	11	12	13	14	15	16
4	17	18	19	20	21	22	23
5	24	25	26	27	28	29	30
6	31						

FEBRUARY

wk	M	T	W	Th	F	S	S
6		1	2	3	4	5	6
7	7	8	9	10	11	12	13
8	14	15	16	17	18	19	20
9	21	22	23	24	25	26	27
10	28						

MARCH

wk	M	T	W	Th	F	S	S
10		1	2	3	4	5	6
11	7	8	9	10	11	12	13
12	14	15	16	17	18	19	20
13	21	22	23	24	25	26	27
14	28	29	30	31			

APRIL

wk	M	T	W	Th	F	S	S
14					1	2	3
15	4	5	6	7	8	9	10
16	11	12	13	14	15	16	17
17	18	19	20	21	22	23	24
18	25	26	27	28	29	30	

MAY

wk	M	T	W	Th	F	S	S
18							1
19	2	3	4	5	6	7	8
20	9	10	11	12	13	14	15
21	16	17	18	19	20	21	22
22	23	24	25	26	27	28	29
23	30	31					

JUNE

wk	M	T	W	Th	F	S	S
23			1	2	3	4	5
24	6	7	8	9	10	11	12
25	13	14	15	16	17	18	19
26	20	21	22	23	24	25	26
27	27	28	29	30			

JULY

wk	M	T	W	Th	F	S	S
27					1	2	3
28	4	5	6	7	8	9	10
29	11	12	13	14	15	16	17
30	18	19	20	21	22	23	24
31	25	26	27	28	29	30	31

AUGUST

wk	M	T	W	Th	F	S	S
32	1	2	3	4	5	6	7
33	8	9	10	11	12	13	14
34	15	16	17	18	19	20	21
35	22	23	24	25	26	27	28
36	29	30	31				

SEPTEMBER

wk	M	T	W	Th	F	S	S
36				1	2	3	4
37	5	6	7	8	9	10	11
38	12	13	14	15	16	17	18
39	19	20	21	22	23	24	25
40	26	27	28	29	30		

OCTOBER

wk	M	T	W	Th	F	S	S
40						1	2
41	3	4	5	6	7	8	9
42	10	11	12	13	14	15	16
43	17	18	19	20	21	22	23
44	24	25	26	27	28	29	30
45	31						

NOVEMBER

wk	M	T	W	Th	F	S	S
45		1	2	3	4	5	6
46	7	8	9	10	11	12	13
47	14	15	16	17	18	19	20
48	21	22	23	24	25	26	27
49	28	29	30				

DECEMBER

wk	M	T	W	Th	F	S	S
49				1	2	3	4
50	5	6	7	8	9	10	11
51	12	13	14	15	16	17	18
52	19	20	21	22	23	24	25
1	26	27	28	29	30	31	

Whale sharks feeding
by Felipe Barrio
Gathered below a school of sardines, these young whale sharks in the Gulf of Tadjoura, near Djibouti are 10 m (30 ft) long. 'We slipped into the water using snorkelling gear and watched them feed, non-stop for three hours. They not only sucked up the plankton, but also the sardines' excrement. It was a fantastic experience.'

Nikon D200 + Nikon 10.5mm lens; 1/50 sec at f4; ISO 160; Seacam housing.

28 *Monday*

29 *Tuesday*

30 *Wednesday*

31 Thursday   *New Year's Eve   Hogmanay (Scotland)   Full moon* ○

Davis', Terry, Kyle, Josh came
over for New year's eve great time

1 Friday   went w/ Nana to   *New Year's Day, Holiday*
beach. All was well, cold

2 Saturday cold, cold!!   **3** Sunday 1st time
Went to GTI   usher as Deacon

January 2010
WEEK 2

Cranes among the corn
by Laszlo Perlaky
These sandhill cranes and snow geese are
feeding in cornfields nearby the Bosque del
Apache National Wildlife Refuge, New Mexico.
'The cranes would slowly walk along the rows,
picking at cobs or corn on the ground. But there
would always be some on alert, craning to look
for coyotes or other dangers.'

*Nikon D2x with 600mm lens; 1/250 sec at f5.6;
100 ISO; Gitzo 1548 tripod with Wimberley head.*

4 *Monday* Holiday (Scotland)

5 *Tuesday*

6 *Wednesday*   *Epiphany (Christian)*

7 *Thursday*

8 *Friday*

9 *Saturday*   **10** *Sunday*

11   *Monday*

12   *Tuesday*

13   *Wednesday*

January 2010

Last of the albatrosses
by Andy Rouse
Steeple Island is a small, uninhabited island in
the Falklands that is home to the world's largest
breeding colony of black-browed albatrosses.
'Sadly few people get to see a large population
of nesting albatrosses. Ten years ago some
200,000 of the birds bred here, but this year I
noticed many of the nests were empty.'

*Canon EOS 1DS Mark II + 24–70mm lens; 1/60
sec at f5.6; ISO 200.*

---

14   *Thursday*   *Makar Sankrant (Hindu)*

---

15   *Friday*   *New moon* ●

---

16   *Saturday*   **17**   *Sunday*

Snowy owl stoop
by Louis-Marie Preau
Louis-Marie took this photograph of a snowy owl in the open fields just north of Quebec. 'It was mid afternoon, and about -15°C. I could see the owl on its nearby perch. Hours later, as the sun set, the owl took off and flew right past me. The magic lasted an instant, but the emotion was intense.'

Canon EOS 1Ds Mark II + Canon 300mm IS f2.8 lens; 1/800 sec at f3.5; tripod.

18   *Monday*   *Martin Luther King Day, Holiday (US)*

19   *Tuesday*

20   *Wednesday*

21 *Thursday*

22 *Friday*

23 *Saturday*   **24** *Sunday*

25 Monday   *Burns Night (Scotland)*

26 Tuesday   *Australia Day, Holiday (Australia)*

27 Wednesday   *Holocaust Memorial Day*

January 2010

WEEK 5

River delta

by Theo Allofs

Theo wanted to show the scale of northern Australia's great Kimberleys wilderness in this aerial shot of a floodplain landscape. 'I was also hoping that I wouldn't fall out of the plane when it banked steeply, so I could photograph looking directly down.'

Mamiya 7 II (6x7 format) with 45mm lens; Fujichrome RVP.

---

28 *Thursday*

---

29 *Friday*

Snow/sleet 8:00pm

---

30 *Saturday*   *Full moon* ○   **31** *Sunday*

snow

no church b/c snow

February 2010

Inquisitive jay
by Jesse Heikkinen
One early morning while Jesse was on a
photography trip with his father to Utti, Finland,
this jay came and perched on the snowy branch
of a pine tree, staring directly into his camera.
'I was so excited to have such long eye-contact
with a wild bird.'

*Nikon D70 with Nikon 70-200mm f2.8 ED VR lens
and 2x teleconverter; 1/320 sec at f5.6; tripod,
hide.*

1 *Monday*

2 *Tuesday*

3 *Wednesday*

4   *Thursday*

5   *Friday*

national board NCAE boot camp

6   *Saturday*   **7**   *Sunday*

national boards boot camp

8 *Monday*

9 *Tuesday*

10 *Wednesday*

Swan lake

by Jan Vermeer

Jan took this photograph by Hokkaido's Lake Kushiro, Japan's largest marshland. 'I wanted different poses of whooper swans in the same frame, set against the white ice. One swan is flying out of frame, another is taking off, three are having a discussion and two are courting – nearly perfect.'

Nikon D2X + 70-200mm lens and 1.4 extender; 1/640 sec at f7.1; Gitzo tripod.

11   *Thursday*

12   *Friday*

13   *Saturday*

14   *Sunday*

St. Valentine's Day
Chinese New Year
New moon ●

February 2010

WEEK 8

The Dark Hedges
by Bob McCallion
A cold, misty February dawn provided the
perfect opportunity to capture this image
of European beech trees, in County Antrim,
Northern Ireland. 'As the sun filtered through the
mist, it bathed the trees in dappled light, giving
the branches form and depth.'

*Fujifilm Finepix S9600 + 28-300mm lens at
300mm and 2x converter; 1/25 sec at f11; tripod.*

15 *Monday*   *Washington's Birthday, Holiday (US)*

16 *Tuesday*   *Shrove Tuesday (Christian)*

17 *Wednesday*   *Ash Wednesday (Christian)*

18 *Thursday*

19 *Friday*

20 *Saturday*   **21** *Sunday*

22   *Monday*

23   *Tuesday*

24   *Wednesday*

Sparring herons
by Bence Máté
When a cold snap froze the lakes near Bence's home in Pusztaszer, Hungary, grey herons gathered where a waterfall prevented an area freezing over. Only a few could fish at a time and, inevitably, squabbles broke out. 'Grey herons maintain their elegance even when arguing.'

Canon EOS 300D with Nikon MF 300mm f2.8 lens and Canon EOS-Nikon converter, Nikon TC-14B teleconverter; 1/2000 sec at f4; hide.

25 *Thursday*

26 *Friday*   *Milad un Nabi, Birthday of the Prophet Muhammad (Islamic)*

27 *Saturday*   **28** *Sunday*   *Full moon* ○

1 *Monday*   *St. David's Day (Wales)*

2 *Tuesday*

3 *Wednesday*

Yawning fox
by Bence Máté
In 2005, an unprecedented amount of snow fell in the Transylvanian mountains. When Bence heard that tourists were feeding a hungry fox from one of the mountain huts, he set off to photograph it. On the fourth day of waiting in the freezing shelter, the fox showed up and he was able to take a series of memorable portraits including this one.

Canon EOS 1N RS with Nikon 300mm f2.8 lens, EOS Nikon converter and Nikon TC-301 2x teleconverter; 1/250sec at f5.6; Fujichrome Velvia 50; Gitzo tripod.

4　*Thursday*

5　*Friday*

6　*Saturday*

7　*Sunday*

8   *Monday*

9   *Tuesday*

10   *Wednesday*

Spring snowflakes
by László Novak
László came across this snowflake plant in spring, in an ancient forest in western Hungary where a river had burst its banks. Though the light was dull, it was ideal for bringing out the white of the petals, contrasting against the soft brown of the water and dark, interlacing network of reflected branches.

Canon EOS 20D with Canon 17-40mm f4 lens; 1/6 sec at f11; 100 ISO; tripod.

11 *Thursday*

12 *Friday*

13 *Saturday*

14 *Sunday*   *Mothering Sunday (UK)*

March 2010

Japanese macaque in blossom
by Yukihiro Fukuda
Yukihiro took hundreds of shots at Jigokudani in Nagano Prefecture before capturing this image of a macaque and cherry trees in spring. 'The macaques are so capricious. It's impossible to predict which tree they will climb next or which flower they will reach for.'

Canon EOS 1D mark II with Canon EF 500mm f4 IS lens; 1/125 sec at f4; 200 ISO; tripod

15　*Monday*　　　　　　　　　　　　　*New moon* ●

16　*Tuesday*

17　*Wednesday*　　　　　*St. Patrick's Day, Holiday (N. Ireland)*

18 *Thursday*

19 *Friday*

20 *Saturday* *Vernal Equinox* **21** *Sunday*

22   *Monday*

23   *Tuesday*

24   *Wednesday*

25   *Thursday*

26   *Friday*

27   *Saturday*

28   *Sunday*   *British Summertime (BST) begins, Palm Sunday (Christian)*

Heart of an agave
by Jack Dykinga
This photograph of an *Agave montana* was taken at sunset
in the mountains of the Sierra Madre Oriental in Tamaulipas,
Mexico. 'The light was extremely low and revealed the patterns
and indentations of each blade.'

*Arca Swiss F-Field + Schneider
Super-Symmar XL 110mm lens; 40
secs at f45; 4 x 5 format Fujichrome
Velvia 50.*

29 *Monday*

30 *Tuesday*   *Full moon* ○

31 *Wednesday*

March – April 2010

Polar trek

by Thorsten Milse

This female polar bear is ravenous, having not eaten for eight months while raising her cubs. Now it is March and she is taking them on a trek to the Hudson Bay to find food. 'You could sense the urgency. The tiny cubs whimpered to their mother as they sank into steep snowdrifts.'

Canon EOS 1DS mark II with Canon EF 600mm f4 IS lens and 1.4x teleconverter; 1/250 sec at f8; tripod.

1   *Thursday*   *Maundy Thursday (Christian)*

2   *Friday*   *Good Friday (Christian), Holiday (UK)*

3   *Saturday*   **4**   *Sunday*   *Easter Sunday (Christian)*

April 2010

Squirrel
by Mart Smit
This squirrel was one of four that played right
in front of Mart's hide in a Norwegian forest. It
suddenly stopped its antics and posed for him in
the early evening light, holding onto a gnarled,
silver stump.

*Canon EOS 10D with Canon 100-400mm lens;
1/250 sec at f6.3; 400 ISO; Gitzo 1228 tripod.*

5   *Monday*   *Easter Monday.   Holiday (UK)*

6   *Tuesday*

7   *Wednesday*   *Last day of Passover (Jewish)*

8   *Thursday*

9   *Friday*

10   *Saturday*   **11**   *Sunday*

12 *Monday*

13 *Tuesday*

14 *Wednesday*   *New moon* ●

April 2010
WEEK 16

Eider lift-off
by Stig Frode Olsen
In the far north of Alaska, Stig watched this male spectacled eider feed, along with its mate. 'I noticed they flew off several times a day to a nearby pond that was fairly ice-free, possibly because they had a nest site close by.' He was soon able to anticipate their departures and so was well prepared for this shot.

Canon 20D with 300mm f2.8 lens and 2x converter; 1/1600 sec at f5.6; 200 ISO; tripod.

15 *Thursday*

16 *Friday*

17 *Saturday*   **18** *Sunday*

19   *Monday*

20   *Tuesday*

21   *Wednesday*

22   *Thursday*

23   *Friday*   *St. George's Day (England)*

24   *Saturday*

25   *Sunday*

Fish round-up
by Alec Connah
These young blacktip reef sharks off Lankayan Island,
near Sabah, Borneo are seemingly herding small fish into
the shallows. 'I liked the patterns that formed as the fish
leisurely evaded them.'

*Nikon F5 + Sigma 70-200mm f2.8
lens; 1/250 sec at f5.6, Fuji Velvia 50
rated at 100 asa*

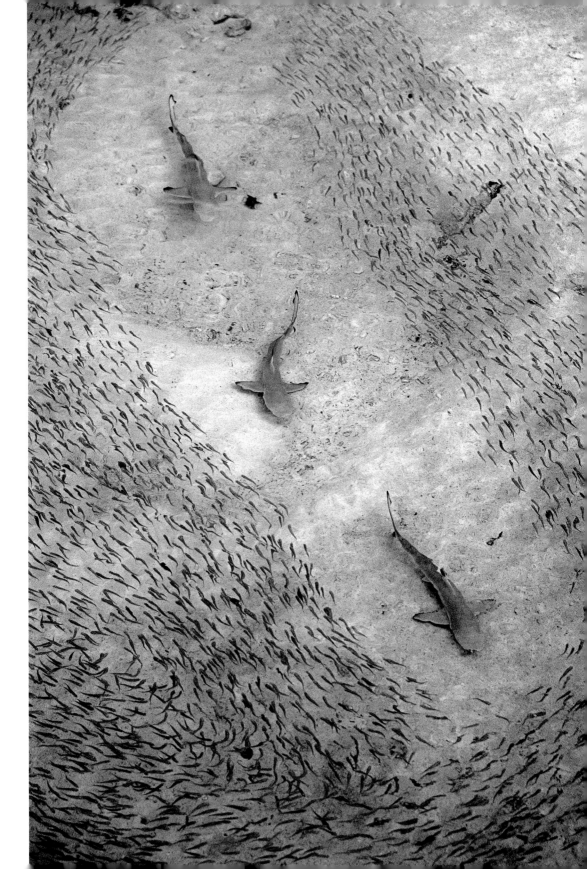

April – May 2010

Penguin in a sand storm

by Martin Eisenhawer

The wind was whipping up sand and grit when Martin took this photograph of a gentoo penguin in the Falkland Islands. 'I stopped where the penguins passed on their way between the colony and the sea and where the peaty ground contrasted with the swirling haze.'

Canon EOS 1Ds Mark II + Canon EF 500mm f4 IS lens; 1/3200 sec at f5; ISO 200; tripod.

26 *Monday*   *Anzac Day, Holiday (Australia)*

27 *Tuesday*

28 *Wednesday*   *Full moon ○*

29   *Thursday*

30   *Friday*

1   *Saturday*   **2**   *Sunday*

3   *Monday*

Early May Holiday (UK)

4   *Tuesday*

5   *Wednesday*

Cinco de Mayo (US)

6   *Thursday*

7   *Friday*

8   *Saturday*

9   *Sunday*

Mother's Day (US & Canada)

Sunlit langur
by Jean-Pierre Zwaenepoel
Jean-Pierre was following a large troop of monkeys in the
Kumbhalgarh Wildlife Sanctuary in Rajasthan, India, when
he spotted this adolescent Hanuman langur 'basking in the
wonderful morning light'.

*Nikon F-100 with 500mm lens; f5.6;
Fujichrome Velvia 100; tripod.*

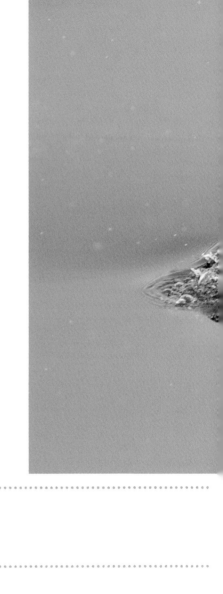

Porpoising penguin
by David Tipling
'It was a particularly dull day for a sail. The sea
became choppy, so I went below deck. But in
Antarctica the weather can change quickly. Ten
minutes later the sea was smooth as a mirror. I
ran back up in time to see this Adélie penguin
leaping across the bow.'

*Nikon D2X + Nikon 300mm f2.8 lens; 1/1000 sec
at f5.*

10   *Monday*

11   *Tuesday*

12   *Wednesday*

---

13   *Thursday*   *Ascension Day (Christian)*

---

14   *Friday*   *New moon* ●

---

15   *Saturday*   **16**   *Sunday*

17 *Monday*

18 *Tuesday*

19 *Wednesday*

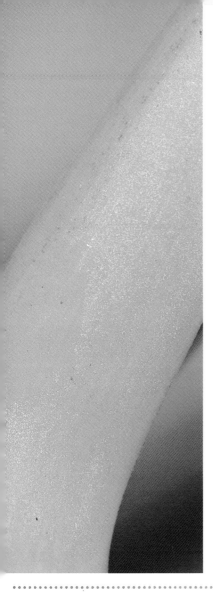

May 2010

Ghost frog
by Edwin Giesbers
Edwin took this photograph of a ghost glass frog in Costa Rica. 'I stood in a stream to get as close as I could. The frog remained motionless as I took its portrait, completely confident in its ability to morph into the plant it was attached to.'

Nikon D70 with Tamron 90mm macro lens; f4; 400 ISO

20 *Thursday*

21 *Friday*

22 *Saturday*

23 *Sunday*   *Pentecost (Christian)*

Cape fox cubs at play
by Helmut Niebuhr
Helmut discovered a den of cape fox cubs in
South Africa's Kgalagadi Transfrontier Park. 'I
visited every day to watch the family. The four
cubs were most active when the light was best
for photography – in the early morning (as here)
and late afternoon.'

*Canon EOS 1D Mark II + 500mm f4 lens; 1/500
sec at f4; ISO 400; beanbag*

24 *Monday*

25 *Tuesday*

26 *Wednesday*

27 *Thursday* *Full moon* ○

28 *Friday*

29 *Saturday* **30** *Sunday* *Trinity Sunday (Christian)*

....

31   *Monday*   *Spring Holiday (UK)   Memorial Day, Holiday (US)*

....

1   *Tuesday*

....

2   *Wednesday*

....

3   *Thursday*   *Corpus Christi (Christian)*

....

4   *Friday*

....

5   *Saturday*

....

6   *Sunday*

Flamingo dance
by Todd Gustafson
This stand of male flamingos at Lake Nakuru, Kenya was
shot from ground level just before dawn. 'I found the
lower down I got, the better the birds looked against the
clear grey sky.'

*Canon EOS 1D Mark II with 600mm
IS lens; 1/1250 sec at f5.6; 100 ISO;
Todd-Pod with a Wimberly head.*

7 *Monday*

8 *Tuesday*

9 *Wednesday*

Mackerel in synchrony
by Béla Násfay
Mackerel usually live out in the ocean, but Béla captured this shot of a huge school in a small area in the Red Sea. 'There were hundreds of mouths agape, moving together as if one. They feasted for three days, which gave me enough time to get to know their behaviour.'

Nikon D200 + AF Micro-Nikkor 60mm f2.8 lens; 1/125 sec at f11; ISO 100; Ikelite housing; 2x DS125 flashes.

10 *Thursday*

11 *Friday*

12 *Saturday*   New moon ●   **13** *Sunday*

14   *Monday*

15   *Tuesday*

16   *Wednesday*

17   *Thursday*

18   *Friday*

19   *Saturday*

20   *Sunday*   *Father's Day (UK & US)*

Butterflies
by Philippe Toussaint
These chalkhill blue butterflies were photographed at the
end of the day in Lorraine, northeastern France. 'I wanted
to capture their jewel-like quality when at rest and spent
time searching for a roost on the chalk grassland.'

*Fujifilm Finepix S2 Pro + AF Micro-
Nikkor 200mm 1.4D lens; 1/125 sec
at f6.7; tripod.*

June 2010

Flower colour
by Maurizio Valentini
Late spring in Abruzzo, central Italy sees
the highlands in full bloom. 'I found this
magic spot with its sea of wildflowers. I
went back many times, waiting for the soft
light of an overcast, rainy day to enhance
the vibrant colours.'

*Hasselblad X Pan II + 90mm f4 lens; 2 secs
at f22; Fujichrome Velvia 50; tripod; cable
release.*

21 *Monday* *Summer Solstice*

22 *Tuesday*

23 *Wednesday*

24 *Thursday*

25 *Friday*

26 *Saturday* *Full moon* ○ **27** *Sunday*

28   *Monday*

29   *Tuesday*

30   *Wednesday*

1   *Thursday*

2   *Friday*

3   *Saturday*

4   *Sunday*   *Independence Day (US)*

Tree frame
by Steffen Sailer
'When I came across this wonderful old plant, I knew I'd
found the image I'd been looking for. The golden-brown
gnarled branches make the perfect frame.' It was taken in
the Quiver Tree Forest in Namibia.

*Canon EOS 1D Mark II with 17-
40mm lens; 1/60 sec at f22; 400
ISO; tripod.*

5   *Monday*   *Holiday (US)*

6   *Tuesday*

7   *Wednesday*

July 2010

Diving tigers
by Elliott Neep
These tiger cubs are playing tiger-tag in Bandhavgarh National Park, Madhya Pradesh, India. 'The cubs were 18 months old, nearly adult, and it got quite rough at times. They chased each other up and down the bank until the first cub dodged and leapt straight into the water, with its playmate in hot pursuit.'

Canon EOS 10D with Sigma 500mm lens; 1/800 sec at f5.6; 200 ISO; Manfrotto 055PROB tripod with 329RC4 head.

8 *Thursday*

9 *Friday*

10 *Saturday*

11 *Sunday*   New moon ●

July 2010

Terrapins on stump
by Manoj C Sindagi
Manoj was running a wildlife photography workshop in Nagarahole National Park, south India when he photographed this scene. 'We were on an evening safari when we came across these sunbathing Indian pond terrapins, necks outstretched, seemingly offering salutations to the sun god.'

Canon EOS 20D with EF 500mm f4 lens and 1.4x teleconverter; 1/320 sec at f6.3; 400 ISO; Manfrotto monopod.

12   *Monday*   *Battle of the Boyne, Holiday (N. Ireland)*

13   *Tuesday*

14   *Wednesday*

15 *Thursday*   *St. Swithin's Day (Christian)*

16 *Friday*

17 *Saturday*   **18** *Sunday*

19 *Monday*

20 *Tuesday*

21 *Wednesday*

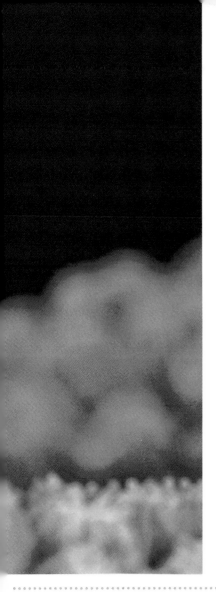

July 2010

Red-lips
by Patrick Weir
The red-lipped blenny is very territorial, and this little fish was darting around its home off Grand Cayman very fast. 'It was difficult to follow with a camera. I managed to get the shot when it paused to look at me. I think it's quite an amusing picture, the way it's looking right at you.'

Nikon D2X + Sigma 28-70mm lens; 1/125 sec at f16; Subal ND2 housing.

22 *Thursday*

23 *Friday*

24 *Saturday*   **25** *Sunday*

Dune

by Bernard van Dierendonck
Bernard took this photograph halfway up Big
Daddy, the tallest of the Sossusvlei Dunes in
Namibia, standing at 325 m (1,070 ft). Below
is Deadvlei, a floodplain plastered with sun-
baked mud. 'The shapes and colours were truly
dramatic. It was nature organised to perfection.'

*Canon EOS 1D Mark II with 24-70mm f2.8L USM
lens; 1/125 sec at f11; 100 ISO.*

26 *Monday*   *Full moon* ○

27 *Tuesday*

28 *Wednesday*

29 *Thursday*

30 *Friday*

31 *Saturday*   **1** *Sunday*

2   *Monday*

3   *Tuesday*

4   *Wednesday*

August 2010

Shy baby
by Kyle Dickerson
Kyle and his parents came across this shy leopard cub hanging around an ant nest in South Africa's Sabi Sands Game Reserve. They all took photographs, keeping as still as possible so as not to disturb it.

Canon EOS 350D with 100-400mm lens; 1/60 sec at f5.6; 200 ISO; beanbag.

5   *Thursday*

6   *Friday*

7   *Saturday*   **8**   *Sunday*

August 2010

Staring black bear
by Thomas Sbampato
This black bear cub in Southeast Alaska's Tongass National Forest was waiting up a tree while its mother went fishing in the nearby salmon-rich waters of the Anan Gorge. While she got busy hooking fish, the cub waited, peering down at Thomas and his clicking camera.

Minolta Maxum 9 with Minolta 400mm f4.5 lens; 1/250 sec at f4.5; Kodak VS 100; tripod.

9   *Monday*

10   *Tuesday*   *New moon* ●

11   *Wednesday*   *Ramadan begins (Islamic)*

12   *Thursday*

13   *Friday*

14   *Saturday*   **15**   *Sunday*

16 *Monday*

17 *Tuesday*

18 *Wednesday*

19 *Thursday*

20 *Friday*

21 *Saturday*

22 *Sunday*

Seascape
by Gary Steer
This beautiful moonlit night is at Coogee Beach near Sydney, Australia. The bands of sky, ocean, surf and sand make it look like a painting. 'Patterns in nature have inspired many impressionist artists, but also photographers.'

Canon EOS 5D + Canon EF 35-350mm lens; 21 secs at f9.9; Manfrotto tripod.

August 2010

The show

by Catriona Parfitt

As this solitary giraffe was walking towards the waterhole at Hobatere Lodge in Namibia it kept looking over towards four lions on a nearby ridge. 'One of the lions, an ambitious young male, raced down from the ridge to chase the giraffe for some distance, watched by the assembled oryx.'

Canon EOS 400D + Canon EF300mm f4 IS USM lens + Canon EF 1.4 extender; 1/200 sec at f5.6; ISO 100.

23   *Monday*

24   *Tuesday*   *Full moon* ○

25   *Wednesday*

26   *Thursday*

27   *Friday*

28   *Saturday*   **29**   *Sunday*

30   *Monday*   *Summer Holiday (UK)   Labor Day, Holiday (US & Canada)*

31   *Tuesday*

1   *Wednesday*

August – September 2010

Swimming for life
by Willem Kolvoort
This newly hatched green turtle on Aldabra
Island, in the Seychelles, was rescued from a pit
which it had become stuck in and released into
the sea. 'I swam out with it, beyond the blacktip
reef sharks I was photographing.'

*Nikon D70 with 10.5mm fisheye lens; 1/800 sec
at f14; 200 ISO; Seacam housing.*

2   *Thursday*

3   *Friday*

4   *Saturday*   **5**   *Sunday*

September 2010

Serengeti stampede
by Liisa Widstrand
Liisa saw this small group of wildebeest start to run in the Serengeti in Tanzania. 'Wildebeest are nervous animals. They run at the slightest threat of danger. It was dusk, and their hooves kicked up clouds of dust that seemed to glow in the evening light.'

Nikon D200 + Nikkor VR 70-200mm f2.8 lens; 1/1000 sec; ISO 100.

6　　*Monday*

7　　*Tuesday*

8　　*Wednesday*　　　　　　　　　　　　*New moon* ●

9 *Thursday*   *Rosh Hashanah (Jewish New Year)*   *Ramadan ends (Islamic)*

10 *Friday*

11 *Saturday*   **12** *Sunday*

13 *Monday*

14 *Tuesday*

15 *Wednesday*

16 *Thursday*

17 *Friday*

18 *Saturday* *Yom Kippur (Jewish)*

19 *Sunday*

Saffrondrop bonnets
by Danny Laps
Danny found these tiny mushrooms in a dark Belgian wood. 'I was charmed by their delicate, glowing colours, softened by the light streaming through the beech leaves. Through my lens it looked like a scene from a child's tale.'

Nikon D200 + 200mm f4 micro lens; 1/6 sec at f6.3; ISO 100; Manfrotto 055 tripod + Arca-Swiss Z1 ballhead.

20   *Monday*

21   *Tuesday*

22   *Wednesday*

23   *Thursday*   *Autumnal Equinox   Full moon* ○

24   *Friday*

25   *Saturday*

26   *Sunday*

Eagle poise
by Robert O'Toole
At the top of an Alaskan ice slope, Robert captured this
photograph of a bald eagle. 'The sun caught the underside
of its wings, and the amazing colour and detail were
revealed.'

Canon EOS 1D Mark II N with an
EF70-200mm L lens; 1/1250 sec at
f4; 200 ISO.

27 *Monday*

28 *Tuesday*

29 *Wednesday*

Bear emerging from water
by Sergey Gorshkov
This brown bear was only a metre (yard) away from Sergey when he noticed it in the Ozernaya River in southern Kamchatka, east Russia. 'It was a terrible shock. I kept calm enough to take the picture but only later did I realise how serious the situation was.'

Nikon D2X + Nikkor 12–24mm f4 G AF-S DX lens at 12mm; 1/250 sec at f10; ISO 200; Subal housing; two strobes INON D2000.

30 *Thursday*

1 *Friday*

2 *Saturday*   **3** *Sunday*

October 2010

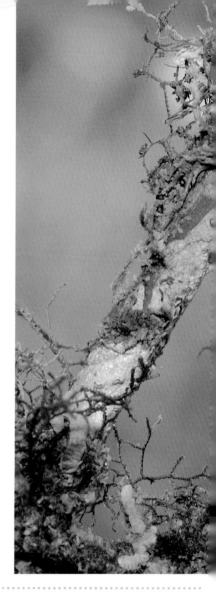

Moss mimic
by Pete Oxford
This katydid was photographed in the
cloudforest of Mindo, on the western slopes
of the Andes in Ecuador. Related to the
grasshopper, it has a camouflage resembling
twigs, moss and lichens and was feeding on the
moss when Pete discovered it.

*Nikon D1x with 105mm f2.8 lens; 1/50 sec at f18;
tripod; flash.*

4   *Monday*

5   *Tuesday*

6   *Wednesday*

7   *Thursday*   *New moon* ●

8   *Friday*

9   *Saturday*   **10**   *Sunday*

October 2010

11 *Monday*

12 *Tuesday*

13 *Wednesday*

14 *Thursday*

15 *Friday*

16 *Saturday*

17 *Sunday*

Mallards at dawn
by Arnaud Darondeau
Arnaud took this photograph of resting mallards on a lake
in central France one chilly October morning. 'I knew just
how magical the light could be at this spot.'

*Nikon D2x with AF-S 500mm f4
lens; 1/250 sec at f11; 200 ISO;
tripod.*

18   *Monday*

19   *Tuesday*

20   *Wednesday*

21   *Thursday*

22   *Friday*   *Wildlife Photographer of the Year Exhibition opens*
                                                                (subject to confirmation)

23   *Saturday*   *Full moon* ○

24   *Sunday*   *United Nations Day*

Vole at the hole
by Danny Green
For the past two years, Danny has been photographing water voles on a disused canal in Derbyshire, UK. 'This one can flood easily, so if heavy rain is predicted, they open the sluice gates to drop the water level.'

Canon EOS 1D Mark II + 500mm f4 lens; 1/100 at f5.6; ISO 400; tripod.

25   *Monday*

26   *Tuesday*

27   *Wednesday*

28   *Thursday*

29   *Friday*

30   *Saturday*

31   *Sunday*   *Halloween   British Summertime (BST) ends*

Daft deer
by Danny Green
Danny had been watching this stag every morning for three
weeks during the autumn rut in Bradgate Park, Leicestershire,
UK. 'When he finally noticed me, he briefly made eye
contact, giving me this mischievous portrait.'

Canon EOS 1V with 500mm IS lens;
1/125 sec at f8; Fujichrome Velvia
50 rated at 80; tripod.

November 2010

Ancient snow gum
by Tom Putt
Tom photographed this snow gum trunk in one of the coldest regions of Australia: Charlotte's Pass, in New South Wales. The size of the snow gum compared to other, thinner trees in the forest suggests it is hundreds of years old.

Canon EOS 20D with EF 17-35mm f2.8 lens; 1/20 sec at f10; 200 ISO.

1   *Monday*   *All Saints Day (Christiam)*

2   *Tuesday*

3   *Wednesday*

4   *Thursday*

5   *Friday*   *Bonfire Night (UK)*   *Diwali (Hindu, Sikh)*

6   *Saturday*   *New moon* ●   **7**   *Sunday*

November 2010

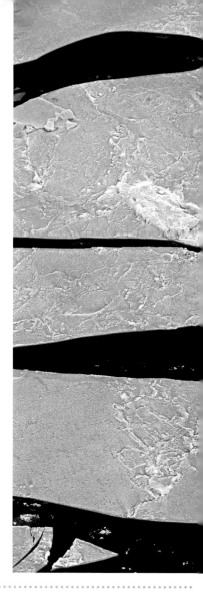

Freezing issues

by Norbert Rosing

These polar bears in the Hudson Bay are hunting on the Arctic ice. 'It was so beautiful, but the cracks in the ice symbolise their future. For two decades, I've visited this place and every year spring has arrived earlier and autumn arrived later.'

Leica R9 with 70–180mm zoom lens; 1/500 sec at f8; gyro stabilizer; Fujichrome Velvia 100.

8   *Monday*

9   *Tuesday*

10   *Wednesday*

11	*Thursday*	*Veterans Day, Holiday (US)*
		Remembrance Day, Holiday (Canada)

12	*Friday*

13	*Saturday*	14	*Sunday*	*Remembrance Sunday*

15   *Monday*

16   *Tuesday*

17   *Wednesday*

18   *Thursday*

19   *Friday*

20   *Saturday*

21   *Sunday*   Full moon ○

Moonrise over badlands
by Franz Josef Kovacs
Franz had a full week to scout the Bisti Badlands in New Mexico for the shot he wanted of the moon rising over the desert horizon. 'I managed to take just two images of the glorious scene.'

Linhof Technikardan 45s + 4x5 Schneider Apo-Symmar 210mm f5.6 lens; 8 secs at f22; Fuji Velvia 50; 0.6 + 0.9 hard-graduated neutral-density Lee filter; Gitzo tripod.

22   *Monday*

23   *Tuesday*

24   *Wednesday*

25   *Thursday*   *Thanksgiving Day, Holiday (US)*

26   *Friday*

27   *Saturday*

28   *Sunday*

Staring gorilla
by Joe McDonald
These mountain gorillas in the Virunga Volcanoes in
Rwanda seemed happy to wait out the day's downpour
in the open. 'I wanted to convey both character and
atmosphere and so zoomed in.'

*Canon EOS 1D mark II with Sigma
120-300mm f2.8 lens; 1/85 sec at
f5.6; 400 ISO.*

29   *Monday*

30   *Tuesday*   *St. Andrew's Day, Holiday (Scotland)*

1   *Wednesday*

Rainforest dawn
by Thomas Endlein
Thomas climbed a 100 m (330 ft) observation
tower at a small research station in Sabah,
Borneo at dawn to take this photograph. 'The
pattern of mist changed so rapidly the view was
never the same from one minute to the next.
I wanted to create the breathtaking mood of
the rainforest.'

*Canon EOS 1N RS with 100-400mm lens; 1/60
sec (+ one f-stop overexposed); Fujichrome Astia
100; tripod.*

---

2 *Thursday* *Festival of Lights, Chanukah (Jewish)*

---

3 *Friday*

---

4 *Saturday* **5** *Sunday* *New moon* ●

December 2010

WEEK 50

Crane in snow
by Tim Laman
When Tim travelled to Hokkaido in Japan to shoot wildlife in the winter, he fell in love with the cranes. 'They look especially beautiful in the snow. I particularly love the way a crane's wings dip delicately as it comes in to land.'

Canon EOS IV with Canon 600mm f4 lens; approximately 1/250 sec at f4; Fujichrome Provia 100 rated at 200; Wimberley-head tripod.

6   *Monday*

7   *Tuesday*   *Islamic New Year (subject to sighting of the moon)*

8   *Wednesday*

9 *Thursday*

10 *Friday*

11 *Saturday* **12** *Sunday*

13   *Monday*

14   *Tuesday*

15   *Wednesday*

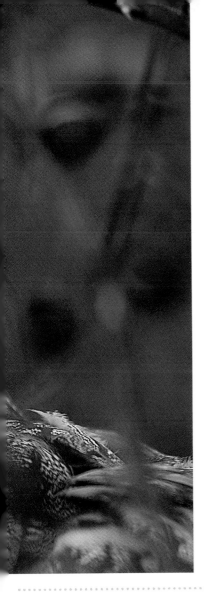

December 2010

Owl glare
by Regis Cavignaux
A group of long-eared owls were dozing in wild rose bushes in Champenoux, France. 'They looked over sometimes, but ignored me. It took me an hour to get close enough, then one turned to look straight at me. Its eyes seemed as bright as the berries.'

Nikon D2Xs + 400mm f2.8 lens; 1/350 sec; ISO 250; monopod.

16 *Thursday*

17 *Friday*

18 *Saturday*   **19** *Sunday*

December 2010

20 *Monday*

21 *Tuesday*

Winter Solstice   Full moon ○

22 *Wednesday*

23 *Thursday*

24 *Friday*

Holiday (US)

25 *Saturday*

Christmas Day (Christian)

26 *Sunday*

Boxing Day

Macaque moment
by Ian Nelson
Ian got very close to this macaque, which sat in warm springs in Jigokudani National Park, Japan. 'There was a sudden commotion between other troop members and it shot a worried glance in the direction of the noise.'

Nikon D2Xs + Nikon VR 200-400mm f/4G lens; 1/200 sec at f/5; ISO 125.

27   *Monday*   *Holiday (UK)*

28   *Tuesday*   *Holiday (UK)*

29   *Wednesday*

Whooper swans at dawn
by Martin Eisenhawer
Martin wanted to frame this peaceful scene of migrant swans in Hokkaido, Japan with an overhanging branch, and spent a long time trying to find the ideal spot. Having found his viewpoint, he had to wait in position until the conditions were perfect to create the picture he had visualised.

Canon 1D mark II with Canon 17-40mm lens; 1/60 sec at f16; 200 ISO.

30 *Thursday*

31 *Friday*   *New Year's Eve   Hogmanay (Scotland)*

1 *Saturday*   *New Year's Day*   **2** *Sunday*

Index of photographers

WEEK 5
Theo Allofs *(Germany)*
theoallofs@northwestel.
net
www.theoallofs.com

WEEK 1
Felipe Barrio *(Spain)*
info@uf-photo.com
www.uf-photo.com

WEEK 51
Regis Cavignaux
(France)
rcavignaux@orange.fr
www.regiscavignaux.com

WEEK 17
Alec Connah *(UK)*
alec.connah@virgin.net
www.latentlight.com

WEEK 42
Arnaud Darondeau
(France)
marie-noelle.darondeau@
wanadoo.fr

WEEK 32
Kyle Dickerson
(South Africa)
Jennette@nelspruiton
line@co.za

WEEK 31
**Bernard van
Dierendonck**
(Netherlands)
bernivd@bluewin.ch
www.vandierendonck.ch
Agent
www.look-foto.de

WEEK 13
Jack Dykinga *(USA)*
jack@dykinga.com
www.dykinga.com
Agents
pete@dykinga.com
www.naturepl.com

WEEKS 18 & 53
Martin Eisenhawer
(Switzerland)
martin@eisenhawer-
naturephotography.com
www.eisenhawer-
naturephotography.com

WEEK 49
Thomas Endlein
(Germany)
te225@cam.ac.uk
www.endlein.org

WEEK 12
Yukihiro Fukuda
(Japan)
fukuda-photo@office.
email.ne.jp
www.fukudayukihiro.com

WEEK 21
Edwin Giesbers
(Netherlands)
info@edwingiesbers.nl
www.edwingiesbers.nl

WEEK 40
Sergey Gorshkov
(Russia)
gsvl@mail.ru
www.gorshkov-photo.
com

WEEKS 43 & 44
Danny Green *(UK)*
danny@dannygreen
photography.com
www.dannygreen
photography.com
Agents
www.rspbimages.com
www.nhpa.co.uk

WEEK 23
Todd Gustafson *(USA)*
gustaphoto@aol.com
www.gustafsonphoto
safari.net

WEEK 6
Jesse Heikkinen
(Finland)
jari.heikkinen@ppq.inet.fi

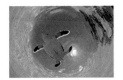

WEEK 36
Willem Kolvoort
(Netherlands)
kolphot@hetnet.nl
www.kolvoortonder
   waterfoto.nl
Agent
www.fotonatura.com

WEEK 47
Franz Josef Kovacs
(Austria)
franz.kovacs@direkt.at
www.kovacs-images.com

WEEK 50
Tim Laman *(USA)*
tim@timlaman.com
www.timlaman.com
Agent
www.ngsimages.com

WEEK 38
Danny Laps *(Belgium)*
dannylaps@skynet.be
www.dannylaps.net

WEEKS 9 &10
Bence Máté *(Hungary)*
bence@matebence.hu
www.matebence.hu
Agent
foto@matebence.hu

WEEK 8
Bob McCallion *(UK)*
mccallion@onetel.com

WEEK 48
Joe McDonald *(USA)*
joe@hoothollow.com
www.hoothollow.com

WEEK 14
Thorsten Milse
(Germany)
info@wildlifephotogra
   phy.de
www.wildlifephotogra
   phy.de

WEEK 24
Béla Násfay *(Hungary)*
nasfay@t-online.hu
www.korallbuvar.hu

WEEK 28
Elliott Neep *(UK)*
Elliott@enwp.co.uk
www.enwp.co.uk

WEEK 52
Ian Nelson *(UK)*
irnelson@mac.com
www.iannelsonwildlife.
   com

WEEK 22
Helmut Niebuhr
(South Africa)
helmutn1@worldonline.
   co.za

WEEK 11
László Novak
(Hungary)
nl@novaklaszlo.hu
www.novaklaszlo.hu

WEEK 16
Stig Frode Olsen
(Norway)
stigfolsen@c2i.net

WEEK 39
Robert O'Toole *(USA)*
rmotoole@gmail.com
www.robertotoole.com

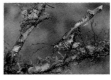

WEEK 41
Pete Oxford *(UK)*
pete@peteoxford.com
www.peteoxford.com
Agent
www.mindenpictures.com

WEEK 35
Catriona Parfitt *(UK)*
cool4cat@btinternet.com

WEEK 2
Laszlo Perlaky *(USA)*
naturalperl@comcast.net
www.naturalperl.com

WEEK 45
Tom Putt *(Australia)*
tom@tomputt.com
www.tomputt.com

WEEK 27
Steffen Sailer
(Germany)
info@sailer-images.com
www.sailer-images.com

WEEK 34
Gary Steer *(Australia)*
gary@wildvisuals.com.au
www.garysteer.com.au

WEEK 7
Jan Vermeer
(Netherlands)
janvermeer.foto@planet.
  nl
www.janvermeer.nl
Agent
www.fotonatural.com

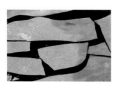

WEEK 4
Louis-Marie Preau
(France)
photo@louismariepreau.
  com
www.louismariepreau.
  com

WEEK 33
Thomas Sbampato
(Switzerland)
thomas@sbampato.ch
www.sbampato.ch

WEEK 20
David Tipling *(UK)*
dt@dtphotos.demon
  co.uk
www.davidtipling.com

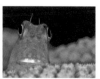

WEEK 30
Patrick Weir *(UK)*
digitaldiver@gmail.com

WEEK 46
Norbert Rosing
(Germany)
rosingbear@aol.com
www.rosing.de
Agents
www.ngsimages.com
www.mauritius-images.
  com

WEEK 29
Manoj C Sindagi
(India)
mcsindhgi@gmail.com
www.manojcsindagi.in

WEEK 25
Philippe Toussaint
(Belgium)
philippe_toussaint@
  skynet.be
www.philippetoussaint.
  com

WEEK 37
Liisa Widstrand
(Sweden)
liisa.widstrand@hotmail
  com

WEEK 15
Mart Smit
(Netherlands)
mart@martsmit.nl
www.martsmit.nl

WEEK 26
Maurizio Valentini
(Italy)
mauvalentini@tiscali.it
www.mauriziovalentini.it
Agent
www.nhpa.co.uk

WEEK 19
**Jean-Pierre
Zwaenepoel** *(Belgium)*
jp.zwaenepoel@telnet.be

First published by the Natural History Museum. Cromwell Road, London, SW7 5BD
© Natural History Museum. London, 2009
Photographs © the individual photographers
Text based on original captions used in the Wildlife Photographer of the Year exhibitions
ISBN : 978 0 565 09240 5

COVER & WEEK 3
Andy Rouse *(UK)*
andyrouse@mac.com
www.andyrouse.co.uk